P9-DNX-358

put the seat down

put the seat down

{ And Other Brilliant Insights for an Awesome First Year of Marriage }

A GUY'S GUIDE

JESS MACCALLUM

Standard®
PUBLISHING

Cincinnati, Ohio

Published by Standard Publishing, Cincinnati, Ohio

www.standardpub.com

Copyright © 2010 by Jess MacCallum

All rights reserved. No part of this book may be reproduced in any form, except for brief quotations in reviews, without the written permission of the publisher.

Also available: *He's Not a Mind Reader and Other Brilliant Insights for a Fabulous First Year of Marriage: A Girl's Guide* by Brenda Garrison, ISBN 978-0-7847-2562-7, copyright © 2010 by Standard Publishing.

Printed in: United States of America

Editor: Dale Reeves
Cover design: Ben Gibson
Interior design: Katherine Lloyd, The DESK
Interior illustrations: Jess MacCallum

All Scripture quotations, unless otherwise indicated, are taken from the *HOLY BIBLE, NEW INTERNATIONAL VERSION®. NIV®.* Copyright © 1973, 1978, 1984 by Biblica, Inc.™ Used by permission of Zondervan. All rights reserved. Scripture quotations marked (*NASB®*) are taken from the *New American Standard Bible®.* Copyright © 1960, 1962, 1963, 1968, 1971, 1972, 1973, 1975, 1977, 1995 by The Lockman Foundation. Used by permission. (www.Lockman. org). All rights reserved. Scripture quotations marked (*NLT*) are taken from the Holy Bible, *New Living Translation.* Copyright © 1996, 2004. Used by permission of Tyndale House Publishers, Inc., Wheaton, Illinois 60189. All rights reserved. Scripture quotations marked (*CEV*) are taken from the *Contemporary English Version.* Copyright © 1991, 1992, 1995 by American Bible Society. Used by permission. All rights reserved. Scripture quotations marked (*The Message*) are taken from *The Message.* Copyright © by Eugene H. Peterson 1993, 1994, 1995, 1996, 2000, 2001, 2002. Used by permission of NavPress Publishing Group.

ISBN 978-0-7847-7462-5

Library of Congress Cataloging-in-Publication Data
MacCallum, Jess, 1964-
   Put the seat down and other brilliant insights for an awesome first year of marriage : a guy's guide / Jess MacCallum.
      p. cm.
   ISBN 978-0-7847-7462-5
   1. Sex role--Religious aspects--Christianity. 2. Marriage--Religious aspects--Christianity. 3. Men--Psychology. I. Title.
   BT708.M28 2010
   248.8'425--dc22
                                        2010001066
15 14 13 12 11 10   1 2 3 4 5 6 7 8 9

To my son,
who I hope will find a girl as great as his mom.

contents

the start is half the deed

"There are two strategies for leading your wife.
I haven't tried either one."

I once heard a pastor say, "Experience is the best teacher, and the best experience is someone else's."

When it comes to marriage, you will learn plenty the hard way, so anything you can learn from some other clueless guy, the better.

I am that guy.

I hope, in the shortest possible time, to stir you up to do better than you would by trial and error, which is man's natural default setting.

In this short book I will be sharing some very simple but practical principles. I'm the first to admit that even with my twenty-two years of married life, I am unqualified to comment as an expert. Not that it would help, since you are not married to my wife, and I am not married to yours. The complete book on *your* successful marriage will be written—literally or figuratively—by you and your wife.

But I do think I can save you some time and trouble. So *initium est dimidium facti*. That's Latin, roughly translated as "The start is half the deed." Let's get busy exploring some principles to help your marriage blast off to a great start.

chapter one

get serious
and get a job

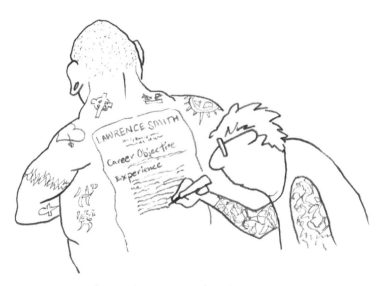

Larry had a hard time holding down a job,
so he always kept his résumé with him.

Despite the self-sufficient, man-bashing characters played by Angelina Jolie, women have a God-given need to be taken care of. They need to feel safe, especially in relationships. No big surprise here for virtually any guy who's paying attention. But where you may not have understood this principle so clearly is in your work and its ability to provide financially. For your wife (and probably her parents), your responsible attitude toward work is a demonstration of your character. It also illustrates your commitment to caring for her day-to-day needs.

Work was God's blessing to man in the Garden of Eden to give him a sense of purpose, provide for real needs, and participate in God's identity as an initiator. Man was intended to follow God's example as an environment maker. God planted a garden and put man in it to tend it (Genesis 2:8, 15), and shortly, God gave him a woman to join his venture and share in its joy.

Of course, that all seems academic on Monday mornings. But that's because Adam turned it into a curse when he sinned. Don't blame Eve entirely for eating the fruit; Adam was right there giving his silent (and taste-testing) approval (Genesis 3:6). Never mind work's ugly side. Being productive at work is still very crucial to a man's spiritual makeup.

Your new wife may not have worried too much about your career choice when she said "I do," but it's your work ethic that will get her attention very quickly—one way or the other. Whether she says it aloud or not, she wants to know you are a hard worker. Ever hear a woman brag to her friends about her husband being fired *again*? Think she wants to bear the financial fallout of a take-this-job-and-shove-it cowboy? Every woman wants to know her man is out there taking care of business—whatever business that might be. This will make you more attractive, I promise. Who knew a work ethic could be sexy?

Let's start with the basics:

- Do you in fact have an honest job?

- Is it forty hours or more a week?

- Does it provide a real paycheck that you can put in the bank?

Sound oversimplified? Believe it or not, there are many men considering marriage who are still living at home and working part-time for their cousin, best friend, or "this guy I know." There's nothing wrong with trying to become a rock star, as long as you do it as a single person. Most men I know can get by with chicken wings (a delicacy in the South), a sofa, and a remote control; most women like a bit more security (not, I emphasize, *luxury*). My wife is not the fur coat and jewelry kind, but she does seem to enjoy food in the refrigerator and running water.

Of course, many newlyweds were both working when they got married, so it didn't seem as obvious a concern.

(Maybe one of you was independently wealthy when you got hitched—which is a whole chapter I am not qualified to write, unfortunately.) But the point here is this: a man who *can* but *doesn't* work and provide financially is undermining his marriage by taking lightly his wife's need for tangible security.

"Oh yeah? Where in the Bible does it say all this?" some slacker with a mild theological interest will ask. Consider these thoughts:

"Now the LORD God had planted a garden in the east, in Eden; and there he put the man he had formed. . . . The LORD God took the man and put him in the Garden of Eden to work it and take care of it" (Genesis 2:8, 15).

———————●———————

"For this reason a man will leave his father and mother and be united to his wife, and they will become one flesh" (Genesis 2:24).

Here from the beginning is the mandate for a man to leave the provision of his father and the caretaking of his mother and establish a household of his own.

———————•———————

"He also gave you manna, a kind of food your ancestors had never even heard about. The LORD was testing you to make you trust him, so that later on he could be good to you. When you become successful, don't say, 'I'm rich, and I've earned it all myself.' Instead, remember that the LORD your God gives you the strength to make a living. That's how he keeps the promise he made to your ancestors" (Deuteronomy 8:16-18, CEV).

God may have given his people manna from Heaven for a while in the desert, but it was his intention to give them real jobs in the promised land.

———————•———————

"Finish your outdoor work and get your fields ready; after that, build your house" (Proverbs 24:27).

In an agrarian society, income derives from the land via farming and livestock. It is wise to establish an income before establishing a permanent residence.

———————•———————

"In the name of the Lord Jesus Christ, we command you, brothers, to keep away from every brother who is idle and does not live according to the teaching you received from us. For you yourselves know how you ought to follow our example. We were not idle when we were with you, nor did we eat anyone's food without paying for it. On the contrary, we worked night and day, laboring and toiling so that we would not be a burden to any of you. . . . We hear that some among you are idle. They are not busy; they are busybodies. Such people we command and urge in the Lord Jesus Christ to settle down and earn the bread they eat" (2 Thessalonians 3:6-8, 11, 12).

The standard for the early church was work, as even the apostles demonstrated.

———•———

"If anyone does not provide for his relatives, and especially for his immediate family, he has denied the faith and is worse than an unbeliever" (1 Timothy 5:8).

Here is the clearest instruction, and one that addresses Christians who were making excuses—possibly spiritual ones—for their deficiencies.

———•———

In college I made a promise to myself that I would have held a real, full-time job for one year before I would marry. (I had Anne in mind, but I wasn't sure she had *me* in mind.) Her father and my father were both WWII

veterans and had worked hard all their lives. I wasn't about
to take on the responsibility of a household without having worked out the issues of basic employment for myself
and for them! I would encourage you to view your job with
the same kind of seriousness. Trust me—it will pay off.

the SMART GUY'S GUIDE to Being Awesome

Here are some practical takeaways to keep in mind as you contemplate your present work situation and future career.

● All honest work is good work, but not all good work pays well. Keep your résumé up to date and always look for something better.

● Don't job hop—it will make your wife nervous and your résumé weak. Don't confuse betterment with your own dissatisfaction.

● Ask your wife what she thinks you could do in your current career, or what else you might do. (My wife's perspective opened up a business career I never dreamed of.)

● Education is important, but it doesn't guarantee a good position. Drive, competence, and good networking are often what make or break your success—with or without higher education.

- Never assume you have to "love what you do" before you take a job, especially in the beginning years. That can be a trap of self-satisfaction, and a hurdle to learning something you might need to know.

  If God does bless both you and your wife with jobs you enjoy and that provide for your family, then you can rejoice with the writer of Ecclesiastes: "It is a good thing to receive wealth from God and the good health to enjoy it. To enjoy your work and accept your lot in life—this is indeed a gift from God" (Ecclesiastes 5:19, *NLT*).

- Don't be afraid to seek counsel from older men who've walked where you are now.

- If you are between jobs, some income is better than none, so do whatever it takes—including temporary, part-time, and even work that you're way overqualified to do—while you look for the right spot.

● Remember the apostle Paul's advice about your work: "Whatever you do, work at it with all your heart, as working for the Lord, not for men" (Colossians 3:23). It's a sound career practice that will get noticed.

chapter two

shut up
and talk

"So . . . how was *your* day?"

I **don't think you will ever** *really* get this. I've been trying for well over twenty years, and I don't have it down. But you need to start somewhere, so here it is: You need to communicate with your new wife by learning to shut up. The things that you've talked about in the past will not be sufficient for your future together. The landscape has changed and new topics are coming. I want to emphasize that from now on, expect "talking" to be unfairly weighted to her subjects.

In some ways, dating has misled us men on this point. Courtship conversations were romantic, spontaneous, exciting, and everything you said was interesting to her. You just knew she was the right girl because she made you feel so "listened to." And it's not that the romance ceases, although if it does slow down, it will be entirely your fault when she brings the topic up . . . but I digress. She has new topics coming online, and you need to practice your shutting-up skills. You must be prepared to value her interest in stuff that is hard to appreciate (commonly referred to as *mind-numbingly boring*). The good news is that *your* limited idea of topics has been abysmally devoid of interest for so long that she's already able to accommodate you, so as a couple you are already halfway to good communication.

This new form of communication will be enriching to her as she gets to talk in journalistic detail about everything your new life together entails. You will be longing to tell her about your latest fantasy football pick. She will want to speculate on the new neighbors, relate an obscure childhood story of little relevance, or plan your fiftieth anniversary. You will be yearning to tell her about the riding mower you sat on at Home Depot last Saturday. She will need to share a brand-new fear she has that no one in the history of rational thought has ever had. You will be dying to jump in and attempt to fix whatever issue she wants to talk through. Simply shut up. She will be *bonding* while she is *talking*. The smart husband will—and I know you will not get this any easier than I have—*get her to talk more*. Ask essay questions. I know the news is about to start, Monday night football looms on the horizon, your boss was in rare form, and the checkbook needs mouth-to-mouth resuscitation—but start to ask questions.

Don't try to fix anything, because it's not broken. At worst it's healing. You don't fix a bruise or cut; you nurse it. Your bride's need to be heard is her way of letting you be the caretaker and confidant others used to be. You are the go-to guy now, the first stop on the list. She may still need to talk to her mother or friends. Just don't *force* her to go to them because you didn't give her the time she needed.

So shut up and talk.

Also beware of the no-topic conversation (not unlike the no-huddle offense in football). That's when she says, "We need to talk," and you will do what we have all done and say, "OK, what do you want to talk about?" This is a trap. She has a topic or six in mind, and it is your job to draw them out, by saying things like . . .

- "OK, I've noticed you seem busier than usual lately."

- "OK, you want to go out for coffee while we talk?"

- "OK, but first I have to apologize for . . ."

Do you see how this avoids putting her on the spot and, instead, gives her a green light to launch whatever's on her mind? When she gets warmed up, just remember not to try and fix her, and don't interrupt, unless it's to ask more questions. If you get this habit down, you will be the smartest guy she ever met. And unbelievable as it may be, you could actually learn something.

James, the Lord's brother, has some great advice for us: "My dear brothers, take note of this: Everyone should be quick to listen, slow to speak and slow to become angry, for man's anger does not bring about the righteous life that God desires" (James 1:19, 20). Wise King Solomon knew something about this as well. And he's the guy who had seven hundred wives and three hundred concubines! He said, "Spouting off before listening to the facts is both shameful and foolish" (Proverbs 18:13, *NLT*).

For most of us guys, listening is not one of our strengths. We tend not to value it as much as we should. Often we are busy formulating our response to something that has just happened or been said.

I love this Bible story from Judges 13:19-23. It deals with Manoah and his wife, who were the parents of Samson the strongman. Upon seeing an angel that had appeared to his wife to foretell the future of Samson, Manoah sacrificed a young goat and brought a grain offering. Then this happened . . .

The LORD did an amazing thing while Manoah and

his wife watched: As the flame blazed up from the altar toward heaven, the angel of the LORD ascended in the flame. Seeing this, Manoah and his wife fell with their faces to the ground. When the angel of the LORD did not show himself again to Manoah and his wife, Manoah realized that it was the angel of the LORD.

"We are doomed to die!" he said to his wife. "We have seen God!"

But his wife answered, "If the LORD had meant to kill us, he would not have accepted a burnt offering and grain offering from our hands, nor shown us all these things or now told us this."

Manoah started off honoring God, but his faith faltered, and he needed his wife to sort out his thinking. Rather than process what had just happened, he felt compelled to verbally respond—and he missed what should have been obvious.

See what you learn when you listen?

Don't get discouraged by thinking that active listening is an Olympic tryout. Your wife is your covenant partner, not an inconvenience. You are doing more than just talking; you're forging your collective identity, you're learning to communicate love, and you're learning what it means to be in partnership. And it might really improve your character development to listen to a creature so different and yet designed to be your suitable helper.

the SMART GUY'S GUIDE to Being Awesome

Your wife needs more than grunts and groans from you. Here are some helpful tips for staying tuned in to your wife's need for authentic communication.

- Be proactive when you come home from work; start the conversation around *her* day.

- See if you can go through one full evening of shutting up and asking questions without offering one piece of unsolicited advice.

- Often the first ten to twenty minutes will be her decompression time. Let her chat about anything without worrying about the content. Be patient; she'll make her point and you'll look really smart.

- Make a short list of topics she is *never* going to want to talk about, such as your kung fu movie collection, how much you *used to* bench press, any old girlfriends . . . Save those topics for wing night with your buddies.

- Watch for signs of listener fatigue to see if you are being just too fascinating for human companionship. Quickly revert to the second bullet point above: ask questions.

- If your wife seems unusually quiet, suggest two or three topics you know she finds interesting, and get her going on one. Or calmly suggest she call her mother.

- Lead her in prayer after she winds down on something that is bothering her.

- Follow up a few days later on one or two specifics she brought up during one of those unloading sessions. (Believe me, she's not done with a subject just because she stopped talking.)

You'll be Husband of the Year if you come back a few days later and show her you are still thinking about something she said—that is, after she picks up her mouth off the floor.

- If you get her talking and it becomes emotionally charged, don't react. It may be difficult to maintain composure, but if you start defending yourself before she's gotten it all out, it will just spiral into an argument. Arguments *can* be therapeutic, but most of the time they don't need to take place.

- If things do escalate into an argument (and they will sometimes), don't ever throw anything in her face that she shared in confidence earlier. Don't quote her to make your point against her. Don't make fun of her. If you do this right, the argument will clear the air and you might even get to make up.

chapter three

she thinks you're still dating

"There you go, dear! I've set a weekly reminder
to be spontaneous and romantic!"

Whether you realized it or not, your wife's catching you was the beginning of *her* permanent social calendar. Yes, an endless lifetime of dating and romance.

A misunderstanding of this will create a generous amount of tension in your marriage—and possibly the common accusation: "He's not the same man I married."

The progression of a woman's thinking is both awe-inspiring and terrifying. Your wife sees everything about you as attached to everything in her world, either supporting or hindering her goals. (If there is going to be a breakthrough in metaphysical thought of any scale, it *will* be from a woman, who will only be understood, sadly, by other women.) In any case, a woman is going to see *your* Friday night, *your* clothes, *your* tone of voice, and *your* job as features of *her* romantic experience.

Of course, men see everything in compartments, ziplocked into easily handled parts, all interchangeable and conveniently unrelated. Here is where romance begins to gasp for air. For you, today is enough to think about; for her, all days exist as one—the one that you are going to set aside to take her somewhere special . . . and listen to her . . . and gaze deeply into her eyes. That's her everyday reality while you and I are checking off our to-do lists and looking forward to *blank* (fill in the *blank* with one of the obvious choices: sex, football, washing the car, going to the gym, or cooking steak on your new grill).

Grasping the difference in how you and your wife view romance is like grasping calculus. Only a few will ever really get it, while most of us will struggle, wondering if the rewards will ever be worth the effort. But since calculus indirectly brought us ESPN, I can assure you that grasping both romance and calculus is *worth it*. If you want to make a huge, positive impact in your marriage, you will not forget the difference in the way men and women process romance . . . nor will you minimize it. You will *not* make excuses about being too tired, you *will* apologize for some comment, or fix that broken lamp, or avoid *whatever* interrupts her vision of the romance you two share. It's a kindness and a real service to her. I know, I know, it can feel unfair; it can feel like a waste of time; it can be frustrating. But if you didn't want a challenging adventure, you should have stayed single and tried something easier like . . . calculus.

In case you're wondering, we'll talk about sex more later on; for now, let's think of the physical component of romance. There are several passages of Scripture that can help us out here. In Genesis 26:7-9, Isaac lied and told the Philistines in the town of Gerar that Rebekah was his sister, because he was afraid that if he told them she was his wife, they would kill him. Apparently, Rebekah was dangerously hot. One particular day, Abimilech, king of the Philistines, looked down from a window and "saw Isaac caressing his wife Rebekah."

Clearly Isaac gave himself away by touching his wife in

a way no one would touch a sister! This was years after he first fell in love with her (Genesis 24:67).

The writer of Proverbs warned that one way to avoid the trap of adultery is to be thrilled with the woman you've married. He gives this instruction to husbands: "May your fountain be blessed, and may you rejoice in the wife of your youth. A loving doe, a graceful deer—may her breasts satisfy you always, may you ever be captivated by her love" (Proverbs 5:18, 19).

If you and your wife haven't read the Song of Songs together, I'd strongly recommend you do so. Part of the dialogue between a husband and wife includes these lines: "Kiss me—full on the mouth! Yes! For your love is better than wine, headier than your aromatic oils. . . . Oh, my dear friend! You're so beautiful! And your eyes so beautiful—like doves! . . . His left hand cradles my head, and his right arm encircles my waist!" (Song of Songs 1:2, 15; 2:6, *The Message*).

But romance is about more than physically touching.

The good news is that you two will probably be doing so much new stuff together that even the little things will seem romantic to her, and you will get some credit to start you off. When I was first married, almost anything I tried seemed to work. But I vividly remember the day the rules changed: I bought her a dress for her birthday that I had picked out all on my own!

Romantic, right? To know your wife's size and taste?

Yes—unless you're still buying styles she wore when you started dating four years earlier and she's a size bigger now. From that point forward, my wife has politely asked for gift cards—and I have happily complied.

Well, that's how we learn and grow.

the SMART GUY'S GUIDE

to Being Awesome

So now you're probably thinking, *What can I do to give her the boost of romance she wants—but at the same time, isn't so much work that I don't quit before I get started?* Here are a few tips.

- Make a short list of the activities your wife enjoys, and scatter them "randomly" in your planner or calendar, at least three months out so you don't have to keep coming up with new things each week.

- Flowers are always a good thing—unless you've borrowed them from a funeral. (Hey, I heard of a pastor who used to do this!)

    Ninety-five percent of women react exactly like the TV commercials suggest they will—all warm and fuzzy and romantic; and an even higher percentage of men seem to forget that flowers work such inexpensive magic. The floral industry generates over $20 billion annually, mostly on last-minute purchases by apologetic or forgetful husbands, who should be using "flower power" on a more regular schedule.

- When you plan an evening out, never make her do your job, which is to actually make some plans. You are not being sensitive to tell her, "It doesn't matter to me . . . anything you want to do." That just says she isn't worth the effort to do it right.

- Endure a chick flick she's been dying to see, without cracking jokes during every corny scene. You never know, she may reward you by watching some ESPN with you or by continuing the movie in the bedroom!

- Do something way out of the ordinary. If you're the stay-at-home types, take a day trip somewhere she's never been. If you're the busy types, spend an entire day together where you can't be interrupted—reading aloud to her, picnicking, and taking it easy.

- Small surprises are amazingly big hits.

- There are a host of tiny things that can mean the world to her: rub her feet without being asked and without trying to turn it into foreplay; make her breakfast; hold her hand; say yes to yet another pair of shoes; compliment her in front of someone else who matters a lot.

- Don't mess up every romantic outing by expecting it to end in the bedroom. Your wife will begin to see your efforts as manipulative, not romantic. This isn't a pay-as-you-go scenario.

- Never, never forget her birthday or your anniversary. Period. No excuses, Jack. They come around on the same day every year.

- Get used to saying "I'm sorry," "You were right," and "Please forgive me." Don't let things build up between you two when all it takes to fix it is a little humility. No amount of the other items above will make up for hurting her feelings and leaving them that way.

chapter four

tell the boys
when to leave

"C'mon, hon, you know Thursday is Frenzy Night!"

Is there anything more annoying and beautiful than a group of men? The loudness, the bodily functions, the need to best each other! It's somehow tribal and necessary for a man to have comrades and competitors all bunched up together and ready to trample the unsuspecting. Glorious.

But keep in mind that your loyalties have changed at the deepest levels. You and your new wife are more than roommates; you have become *one flesh,* a new identity. She may not find your friends as entertaining as you do, and definitely will not have the hours upon hours of tolerance for their company. She married you, not them—as much fun as they may be. But not to fret. Most wives are OK with the gang coming by . . . at scheduled times . . . with an exit strategy. You may even have friends in common from the days when you were dating. But it's your responsibility to make sure her environment is not overrun with Larrys and Daves and Ralphs. They may be great guys, but don't let them overstay their welcome.

If you are a sports guy, a fraternity guy, a poker guy, a video game guy, a hunting or fishing guy, you will have to be on extra alert. These are functions built for masculine camaraderie, and once the testosterone level is heightened, it's hard to think clearly. This is where clear prior communication will help avoid annoyed pals or, worse, an irritated wife. Don't ever forget that no matter how late they stay, you will be facing her when they finally do leave. It's disloyal to always put your wife in the position of saying when enough is enough.

I knew a young man who got engaged to a wonderful girl introduced to him by his best friend. Naturally, the young man thought it was cool to include his best friend on many of their dates. Actually, *most* of them. That lasted until all their other friends began joking that they couldn't tell which one the young man was engaged to. To the girl's credit, she never nagged him about it, but I'm not sure she would have gone to the altar had there not come a point where *she* became his *new* best friend.

Of course, you will not always know when some of the fellows might drop by unannounced and want to hang out. This is a good time to be more of the alpha dog than they are and mark your territory.

A man who will not tell people in his own house what is acceptable and what is not won't have much of a home left before long. This includes telling friends and family when the evening is done. Be tactful of course. Just never, and I repeat *never,* hide behind your wife's displeasure. Don't insinuate that she's getting tired of them and will take it out on you later. That's disloyal, and it makes you look weak as well. If ever you have a choice to accommodate either friends and family or your wife, believe this one thing—she'd better win. Treat her with deference first to safeguard and establish the bond of marriage. Even if you think she is wrong or could have been more understanding, deal with those issues separately. Don't make it worse by choosing anyone else over your wife. She may actually be right, and you just can't see it yet. You can send me a thank-you note later.

Here are some appropriate Scriptures on the topic of where your loyalties should now lie:

"A man leaves his father and mother and is joined to his wife, and the two are united into one" (Genesis 2:24, NLT).

"Many a man proclaims his own loyalty, but who can find a trustworthy man?" (Proverbs 20:6, NASB).

And a woman is always asking this question!

"Husbands, in the same way be considerate as you live with your wives, and treat them with respect" (1 Peter 3:7).

t's all a matter of priority. Most men seem to get this whole thing the hard way, after the silent treatment or several arguments. Ultimately, you can choose whether this will be a source of great tension or a means to build intimacy by reinforcing personal loyalty. Here are some helpful ideas you can practice—starting today.

- Let your friends know that just dropping by isn't going to cut it anymore. Make sure they call first.

- Communicate to everyone, especially your family, that your status has changed and there is no competition with your new wife when it comes to priority.

- Schedule a night (with your wife's OK) to have the boys over. If you have masculine interests that are difficult for your wife to tolerate—like cranking up high-decibel music, hurling insults at the basketball refs on TV, or examining Jason's newly bagged buck . . . with bullet holes—maybe you can host this event somewhere other than the living room.

- You could also encourage your wife to set a time to go out with her friends or have them over for a girls' night. Hey, you could even be the cook or waiter for them!

- Whenever you make social arrangements with your wife, remember two things:

  1. Make sure her agreement is totally voluntary.

  2. Check in with her once in a while to make sure she hasn't changed her mind. Things can and do change.

- If you have clueless friends, difficult family members, or intrusive in-laws—(like any of *those* could ever become a possibility!)—you may want to sit them down privately and explain the new lay of the land. It should go something like this: "I put my wife first in my house. This little chat is my idea, and I'd like you to have time to adjust so that I don't ever have to embarrass you at a social function—because I will *never* take your side over my wife's."

chapter five

put the
seat down

"Yes, dea—uuuggGGHHHHH!"

It's the little things that separate us from the lower animals, in addition to opposable thumbs and an eternal soul. From the common courtesy of holding a door open to the conscious self-sacrifice of forfeiting the last piece of cake, this is the stuff great men are made of. At least, great to your wife.

The greatest consideration of all is one I had to learn from an older, wiser man. He told me to put the seat down on the toilet so my wife wouldn't have to do it.

That's it.

Sounds trivial, but the first time your new wife sits in a bowl of cold water in the middle of the night, you'll wish you had a couple of roommates to blame. But you won't. And you know, if you make a habit of that kind of thoughtlessness, it might take several gifts of flowers, chocolate, and shopping trips to bring your universe back into balance.

During our first five years of marriage, Anne and I moved about every year, upgrading from one apartment to another. I'm a creature (though not a slave) of routine, and I like certain personal things left alone; namely, which side of the bed I sleep on. But my new wife prized one thing above all else in her bedroom arrangement: she wanted to be able to see the moon at night from bed. So wherever we moved, I took the side that *couldn't* see the moon. I had to readjust—and try not to crash into the furniture at night on the way to the bathroom.

If Anne and I had been living during the days of Moses, I would have had a whole year to learn how to take care of her needs and make her as happy as possible. The law stipulated, "If a man has recently married, he must not be sent to war or have any other duty laid on him. For one year he is to be free to stay at home and bring happiness to the wife he has married" (Deuteronomy 24:5). Wow, that's consideration!

Consideration is a mind-set. Even though it can be

confused with manners and upbringing, it comes from the very root of being a man. Adam, our great-great-great-etc-grandfather (you do the math), was given an implicit task when he got his new wife Eve: he was to *remember* God's ordinances and teach his wife what God expected of them both, concerning the tree of the knowledge of good and evil. God never directly told Eve not to eat of the tree; he only told Adam. Eve hadn't been created yet (Genesis 2:17, 18). Adam was responsible to remember and communicate. And even though he started well (Eve accurately answered the serpent's question in Genesis 3:3), things didn't end so well when it was crunch time—even though Adam seems to have been *standing right there!* (v. 6).

So now it's intrinsic to us husbands to also fail at this task. But it's part of the deal, and we should make the effort to study our wives and treat them with consideration and kindness. It will have a great effect on your own character as a servant and a leader, and according to Scripture it will even help your personal prayer life (1 Peter 3:7).

When speaking about the kind of attitude believers should show toward others, Paul challenged his readers to "do nothing from selfishness or empty conceit, but with humility of mind regard one another as more important than yourselves" (Philippians 2:3, *NASB*). If others outside your marriage are supposed to receive this kind of consideration, how much more should your wife!

Paul also spoke these directives to husbands:

Husbands, go all out in your love for your wives, exactly as Christ did for the church—a love marked by giving, not getting. . . . And that is how husbands ought to love their wives. They're really doing themselves a favor—since they're already "one" in marriage. No one abuses his own body, does he? No, he feeds and pampers it. That's how Christ treats us, the church, since we are part of his body (Ephesians 5:25, 28, 29, *The Message*).

How are you doing with "going all out in your love" for your wife—feeding and pampering her? It's all a part of showing her consideration.

By the time you get married, you've had a few chances to learn the hard way: forgotten occasions, careless comments, missed opportunities. And in your new life together you will have *endless* chances to learn the easy way—if you so choose. If you develop a servant attitude in the small areas, it will communicate love and concern daily, and will save you a small fortune in flowers-and-chocolate apologies.

the SMART GUY'S GUIDE **to Being Awesome**

f you want to get an A on your report card for showing consideration, here's how it's done.

- Learn to put the seat down on the toilet. It's an easy habit to develop and one for which you will be appreciated. You're no longer living in a guys' dorm.

- While you're in the bathroom, don't leave an empty roll on the toilet paper holder. Make sure there's a clean towel left for your wife, and rinse out the sink after you shave. All without being asked to!

- Assign yourself the chores she hates the most, even if you hate them too. Taking out the trash, cleaning up after dinner, scrubbing toilets, cleaning the cat litter box, whatever. In this small way, you will be the knight in shining armor. To the rescue!

- Pick up her stuff as well as yours. It's easy to say that you pick up after yourself, but that just makes you a well-raised ten-year-old child. A considerate husband picks up after his wife as well.

- Open the car door for her when you go out—even when *she's* driving.

- Make a note of all special occasions on your calendar for the year, and maybe a note to remind yourself a week ahead.

- *Never* make fun of her in public; you'll pay for it in private.

- Whatever she's sensitive about is off limits for joking. Never drag one of these areas out to use in an argument either. It's insensitive, and you will only dig a deep hole for yourself to get out of.

- Do a little investigation before you "help" her. She may have reasons for not wanting you in her kitchen, or planning surprise getaways, or buying her a clothes item that you think she needs.

● Ask her opinion often—you might even learn something.

chapter six

it may be your castle, but it's her nest

"You know, I think the wide screen really *makes* the place."

The task of integrating two people into the kind of unity God intended is similar to a Siamese twin separation operation—only in reverse. The process takes a ton of effort, but the result is a new, more fulfilling life. It is a spiritual adventure, but has a very material aspect—or two.

The idea that a man and woman "become one" when they are married was introduced by God in the Garden of Eden. But as soon as cultures graduated from tents and caves to houses, women began to realize they were going to be staying put for a while. This ultimately led to Martha Stewart–type closet organizers and a concept called decorating. It may have been *his* house, but it was *her* home. The nesting instinct grew in her, and he rebelled by leaving his work shoes/sandals/moccasins wherever he darn well pleased.

Things are not much different even today. A shared life requires a shared environment and a shared—or at least negotiated—set of sensibilities. It doesn't do much good to one's marriage to debate every stick of furniture, carpet texture, or room color. This is where you as a leader step up to the plate and do the thing that hurts. This might mean sacrificing some of your "cool" stuff.

Yeah, most of us men thought our sense of space and decor was *groovy* before we got married. I certainly thought my eclectic '80s style would be appreciated. Found stuff, inherited stuff, and more found stuff built a wonderful neo-suburban post-college experience for anyone able to grasp it. But with marriage came enlightenment, and the opportunity to show my love for my new wife in a painfully material way. First to go was the cinder block and plank shelving she thought was too "dorm-ish," despite its gritty masculinity. Also all posters push-pinned to the wall and anything won at the state fair. Even some very collectible antiques were abandoned because they presented a "health threat"—whatever that meant.

Her stuff was mostly OK by definition. It was stylish

and clean. My argument that "stained or melted items can still be clean" fell on deaf ears; that "thrift store flatware is eclectic" went nowhere; that "irregular pieces of shag carpet can, in fact, be classified as throw rugs" was ignored.

So here's the point: she needs to nest, and you need to sacrifice.

As mentioned in chapter 1, man (and more particularly, a husband) is supposed to be an environment maker. That's not just some vague spiritual metaphor without connection to your dirty socks. Your sacrifice will go a long way to making your new wife feel secure and comfortable. If you truly understand her need to build her personality into her environment, this will help you avoid feelings of intrusion or resentment as she tosses out your junk. And most importantly, you will have taken the road less traveled to a peaceful home.

Scripture has something to say about your wife's need for nesting. Here are a few examples:

"The wise woman builds her house, but with her own hands the foolish one tears hers down" (Proverbs 14:1).

"She carefully watches everything in her household and suffers nothing from laziness. . . . Reward her for all she has done. Let her deeds publicly declare her praise" (Proverbs 31:27, 31, NLT).

"These older women must train the younger women to love their husbands and their children, to live wisely and be pure, to work in their homes, to do good, and to be submissive to their husbands. Then they will not bring shame on the word of God. In the same way, encourage the young men to live wisely" (Titus 2:4-6, NLT).

Before you use the submission part of this verse like a weapon, you might want to "live wisely" when your wife donates your junky furniture to a thrift store. After all, she is commanded by God to do it . . . sort of.

———————•———————

OK, admittedly the Bible does not have much counsel on home decorating. HGTV and the DIY Network did not exist when the Bible was written. But the principles from the verses referenced above apply in this arena. A husband's first priority in ancient Israel, even above national defense, was to make his new wife happy.

Supporting your wife's natural desire to create a comfortable haven is a good practical place to start. And if you will let her do her thing, you will find the environment is better for you as well—and she might even let you be the king of your garage or other manly space. Because you can still dream, check out the decor of man caves that are sometimes featured at www.hgtv.com and www.diynetwork.com.

the SMART GUY'S GUIDE to Being Awesome

L et your wife know up front that her tastes will be honored above yours. This is probably a lot easier than it sounds, since most guys have little to no taste anyway.

- Listen to her rationale for her choices, because most new wives are as eager to please their new husbands as they are to decorate. She has her reasons, so try to at least sound interested. You might even learn something.

- Don't be a tightwad. Even on a slim budget, you can afford to do some sensible decorating. Remember, it's a priority for her to build a nest and an identity for your new life together, so don't nickel and dime her. You'll reap the return on the investment.

- When guests come over, you should point out how well your

new wife has done. Even brag a little, especially to your own mother, so your wife knows you are together on this issue— and so does everyone else.

● Rearranging the furniture is part of the deal, so don't balk at moving stuff back and forth until she decides it's right.

● If she has some odd tendencies with color or style, *cautiously* encourage her to subscribe to a decorating magazine to . . . *ahem,* sharpen her sensibilities.

● Don't get bent out of shape if she rejects your stuff. That's what attics, basements, and storage bins are for. You might be able to negotiate a small space for yourself, like a man cave or study.

● If you are the rare man who knows decor and color, maybe even architecture, be careful not to outdo your wife. She still needs her say, and you will have to take more care to shut up and listen as your natural confidence will want to "win" room by room. In fact, you may want to butt out entirely so she can feel freer.

chapter seven

holy sex!

"I knew you were a Puritan when I married you. But honestly, Henry, do you ever think about anything besides sects, sects, sects?"

Let's cut to the chase: most men are engrossed with the subject of sex. This comes from both good and bad desires—the creative intimacy of the God-given vs. the destructive self-absorption of the flesh. The problem in our society is that the flesh's version of sex gets top billing. (I always laugh when celebrities decry the "Puritan ideals" that still make America "sexually repressed." What America are *they* living in? They act as if everywhere outside Hollywood is all Amish country.) Like it or not, the topic of sex is thrown at you from virtually every direction, and with ever-increasing intensity—wrapped around every conceivable product, sitcom, and interview. And to be honest, most of us don't try exceedingly hard to avoid it. That's going to be a problem when you get married. The volume of unlearning we must do is far greater than most of us imagine.

Speaking of things to undo, I should pause here to speak bluntly about sex before marriage. Don't do it. Don't get close to doing it. Don't put yourself and your beloved in a compromising situation where a crowbar wouldn't separate you. You are going to rob your wedding night of its intended ecstasy, and make your first year harder than you would guess. Of course, if you have no interest in Christlikeness, this sounds like a ridiculous restriction to your natural passions. However, on the assumption that the Bible does mean something to you, and you want to lead your bride spiritually, then lead *away* from the edge of disobedience, not toward it to see how far you can lean over before you fall.

I'm not naive. I know a large number of Christian couples have developed active sexual behaviors before they entered into marriage. These habits leave their mark. Proverbs 6:27 warns, "Can a man scoop fire into his lap without his clothes being burned?" You can't develop sexual habits before marriage that won't come back to cause you grief. Even within marriage, some sexual things tear down and some build up.

If you have become physically intimate with your fiancée or girlfriend, it may not be too late to salvage things, but you'd better get some outside accountability. A pastor, a mentor, or even a trusted friend can help you straighten out the crooked thinking. You will need to make some decisions about how you will continue with the relationship on a God-honoring course that will last into your marriage. If you are already married and you have a history of sex before marriage, then I seriously suggest counseling to work out any issues of lingering guilt or self-centeredness in the bedroom.

Our society's overindulgence in sexuality has poisoned us, numbing the desire (even of Christians) to pursue real holiness in the bedroom.

And there's no better example of the poison of this world than pornography. It's virtually the foundation of the Internet, trapping even well-intentioned Christian men, daily, in an addiction that no previous generation could have imagined. It's not only available but also aggressively seeking you and me . . . and our wives. Don't be misled about pornography. It is a thief that comes "only to steal and kill and destroy" (see John 10:10) your marriage and your walk with God.

If you struggle with the Internet, cable or satellite TV, or even the eye-popping covers of certain magazines, you need a brother to confide in, to hold you accountable, and to pray with you (not just pray *for* you). And maybe you should cancel your subscription to 687 channels of tempting movies. Maybe checking your eBay account late at night is a bad idea. Maybe you need to pluck out your "eye" (your online "eye") if it causes you to sin (Matthew 18:9).

Maybe it's time to get *ruthless*, especially if you've developed a habit as a single man. Because as a married man, you won't be poisoning just yourself; you'll be bringing that into the life of the woman you love. You both need the blessing of purity in the bedroom.

Christ followers are challenged with these words: "You must live as God's obedient children. Don't slip back into your old ways of living to satisfy your own desires. You didn't know any better then. But now you must be holy in everything you do, just as God who chose you is holy. For the Scriptures say, 'You must be holy because I am holy.'" (1 Peter 1:14-16, *NLT*). To be *holy* means not only to seek purity but also to be "set apart" from what is common. By God's definition, your sex life should be uncommon. Unfortunately, the creative power of sex is often lost on concerns about technique, self-satisfaction, and performance. In contrast to the world's agenda, the Christian marriage bed should be the place where you bring the metaphor of oneness to a reality unattainable by the nonspiritual world.

The Genesis account shows that God's original design for companionship was so that man and woman would experience unity or, technically, re-unity—since the woman came from the man and was, therefore, the proverbial perfect fit. Genesis 2:23, 24 says, "The man said, 'This is now bone of my bones, and flesh of my flesh; she shall be called Woman, because she was taken out of

Man.' For this reason a man shall leave his father and his mother, and be joined to his wife; and they shall become one flesh"(*NASB*).

The good news about this kind of holy sex and "oneness" is that the rewards are better than anyone has ever told you. Most guys do not compare their married sex lives with that of their buddies, but women do not always feel that same hesitation in sharing with their friends. If you take the time to make your bed a place where your wife looks forward to meeting you, her friends may ask you to give a seminar to their husbands. In addition to her confidence in you growing, your confidence in yourself will be at an all-time high. Peace in your thought life will increase, and temptation will begin to pale in comparison to the deep emotional needs that will be met in you both.

It's not magic, just a strong dose of the reality you are supposed to enjoy together.

Will you be a leader who is committed to your bride the way Christ is committed to the perfection of his church? If so, take a look at Christ's unconditional love; he's unselfish and patient—two traits that will set apart your sex in the bedroom. Here are some more directives from Scripture that will help you experience holy sex:

"For the mind set on the flesh is death, but the mind set on the Spirit is life and peace" (Romans 8:6, NASB).

Try adding the words *in the bedroom* to the middle and end of that verse. Believe me, when you approach sex God's way, you will appreciate life and peace far longer than the temporary thrill of the flesh—and the lingering guilt that comes with it.

———•———

"Give honor to marriage, and remain faithful to one another in marriage. God will surely judge people who are immoral and those who commit adultery" (Hebrews 13:4, NLT).

"Sexual drives are strong, but marriage is strong enough to contain them and provide for a balanced and fulfilling sexual life in a world of sexual disorder. The marriage bed must be a place of mutuality—the husband seeking to satisfy his wife, the wife seeking to satisfy her husband. Marriage is not a place to 'stand up for your rights.' Marriage is a decision to serve the other, whether in bed or out" (1 Corinthians 7:3, 4, The Message).

Don't get confused at this point. Sex should be both spiritual *and* great fun. A healthy sex life takes the edge off just about every other topic or issue between you and your wife. And it's the husband's job to keep the marriage bed a refuge for both partners, a place she looks forward to being with you—not a place where she suddenly gets "a headache."

One last comment: if you marry a woman who has a stronger sex drive than you, then you will have some unique challenges. (Lucky dog.) It will take some sensitive communication from you to assure your new wife when she feels any reluctance on your part. You will also have to train yourself to be intimate at a pace closer to what she enjoys, as a loving husband if not an aroused one. It's not abnormal even if it's unusual; each marriage has its shape and tone sexually, but each is God-given and intended to be honoring to him.

the SMART GUY'S GUIDE to Being Awesome

● If you haven't done so already, get rid of anything in your bedroom that conforms to the world's idea of sexuality, including
books and movies. (Well-meaning secular books on sex can
miss the whole oneness-of-spirit thing.)

● I strongly urge you to remove any television from the bedroom.
It's tied straight to the world and can fill the quiet moments you
could be sharing.

● The optimum word in the bedroom should be *respect*. No
pressure, no uncomfortable experimentation, no language you
wouldn't want your wife to tell her friends. As long as you both
are respectful of each other, you will naturally gravitate toward
an unequalled sex life.

- Start foreplay seventy-two hours in advance of sex. She'll be tearing your clothes off by the time the door is shut.

- Think about the mood. The one *she* would like. Music, lighting, a clean husband.

- If you can't remember anything else, take my dad's advice— which he gave me five minutes before my wedding started: "Take your time, son. You'll be fine."

- Men frequently miss the point of the time commonly known as afterglow. Women expect it, and men need it more than they know. Take time after sex to just be together, and you will bond faster, be less tempted by outside influences, and improve your next experience in the bedroom.

chapter eight

how many in-laws does it take to change a lightbulb?

"My in-laws and I were happy for many years . . .
then I married their daughter."

How many in-laws does it take to change a lightbulb? No one knows yet, because half of them are still arguing and the other half won't speak to each other.

OK, I'm *mostly* joking.

For most of us guys, marrying our new bride means marrying into a family. And this new family has expectations—realistic or not—and a whole lot of time and energy invested into that little princess you are rescuing from the tower. They have opinions and feelings and all manner of reasons to stick their noses in.

Of course, there are good in-laws too, but they are mostly comprised of us. We guys assume we are the best addition to someone else's quirky family, right? Our mere addition raises the average IQ, refreshes the gene pool, and puts the clan on the map. Maybe the other side gets this, and maybe they don't. It will be a wonderful experience discovering all the nuances of dysfunctional relationships you have entered into, and a little terrifying facing the ones that you brought from home.

Again, I am *mostly* joking.

Genesis 2:24 mandates that you leave the provision of your father and the caretaking of your mother and establish a household of your own. Hopefully, it does not require alienating your parents to do it. I know there are exceptions, but almost all new couples bring a set of in-laws into the mix. She gets to know your side, and you get to know hers. No doubt you've scoped out most of these people before the wedding. If not, you may want to tear this chapter out and tape it to the bathroom mirror, because *stuff* is coming. In any case, much of what you will face as a couple from the various interested parties will come out only after the knot is tied. That's because everyone's facade is going to begin to melt away. People, including you and your wife, are complex, frail, noble, and above all, different from each other. And thanks to marriage, they are allowed to rub you the wrong way in a manner they didn't when you were dating or engaged.

First big point I need to make: *never* compare members from both of your families. This isn't a dog show with points off for flaws in perfection. You and your new wife have begun a brand-new family, and together you will set new rules for dealing with the inevitable conflicts of satisfying a lot of well-meaning screwed-up people. If your mother is like Mother Teresa (if she hadn't been a nun), don't ever hint that your wife got the better end of the deal. Don't mention your uncle, the Nobel Prize–winning psychiatrist, every time your wife's sister checks back into rehab.

Second big point I need to make: don't get dragged into a fight that isn't yours. If there's conflict in the extended family, remember that you and your wife are one, and you will handle all extended conflicts as *outside* conflicts. In many cases your involvement will not change the outcome anyway and will exhaust you both—leading to conflict *inside* your marriage.

Let's pretend that you both have reasonable sides and

that they get along with each other. And you and your wife have perfect communication. (I said we're pretending here.) Your first holiday season as a married couple is fast approaching. Both sides of the family are big on Thanksgiving, and they live too far apart to split the holiday. Feel the tension already, don't you? You are going to disappoint one side or the other. Do you trade off Christmas or New Year's Day? Do you stay put and make them all come to you? (Pretending again.) Do you disappear to Cancun? (Several movies have been made about this option.)

Some young couples will have two sets of remarried parents and two single parents (alone on the holidays!) to make this dilemma feel like a torturous algebra exam. The way you work through these very real, very sensitive situations will be a signal to your extended families of how much you respect them and desire to include them (assuming you do). Even under perfect circumstances, there will be tough choices to make. These will not always be as simple as holiday logistics. Things like . . .

- Will you hire your brother-in-law?

- Will you work for your father-in-law?

- Is your father's second wife welcome to family functions?

- When your wife's mom starts lecturing you over dinner, how will you handle it?

The list goes on. And just wait until you start having kids!

There is a rare exception to the above conundrum: totally absent in-laws. You might have married a girl whose parents have died or, due to the fracturing of a family, have just sort of fallen off the radar. With the rate of divorce and remarriage today, some newlyweds end up surrounded by strangers at family reunions—if you can find enough people to show up for one. Or it might be *you* without a "side of the family" to bring to the table, for the same reasons. This will have some issues that are unique. If your wife has been without a mom for years, and yours isn't what she'd always hoped for, you'll need to work through your bride's disappointment. Or you might not have gotten the brothers you never had, because hers don't care about anything but themselves.

There's always the possibility that the mother and father and brothers and sisters you've gained are better than you originally had in your family. Moses lived and worked for his father-in-law, Jethro, for forty years as a shepherd—and apparently found the kind of second father we'd all love. When Moses needed some solid advice, he received it from Jethro, and "Moses listened to his father-in-law and did everything he said" (Exodus 18:24).

After both her sons died, Naomi tried to send her daughters-in-law back to their families, but Ruth would not go. She said, "Where you go I will go, and where you stay I will stay. Your people will be my people and your

God my God" (Ruth 1:16). Ruth formed a great bond with her second mother that even the death of her husband could not break.

With good in-laws you may gain the father you never had, and your wife may find what she's always wanted—a sister to talk to. If so, give thanks to God, tear out this chapter, and give it to some poor guy whose marriage is besieged by her tribe.

You will, however, still have to deal with the holiday issue!

You would do well to avoid emulating the example of Jacob and his uncle/father-in-law, Laban, which is recorded in Genesis 29–31. This is one of the most detailed cases in Scripture of how family relations can strain over time. Take a few minutes to read those chapters. I'll wait.

Incredible, huh? What started out as a very happy relationship deteriorated over the years through mutual deception, anger, and fear. But your relationships don't have to be like that—and at least you didn't have to work for your father-in-law for fourteen years to get your bride!

In-laws come with the deal almost every time. And as the new head of a new household, you will have to lead your wife—gently, protectively, sacrificially—through the complexities of managing a host of new issues. Respect for the larger family is key, but being united in your approach is critical. The essential thing is to stand together on the issues that extended family brings. Being respectfully independent is a feature of a healthy Christian marriage. It's our job to lead and to learn.

the SMART GUY'S GUIDE to Being Awesome

- Be honest with each other about your feelings toward your future or new in-laws. Respectfully. One day you may be someone's parents-in-law.

- Well in advance of all special events and holidays, take out a calendar and discuss your desires first, then the expectations of your extended families.

- Honoring your new side of the family should be a goal for each of you and should include some individual time with your new in-laws. (I went with my father-in-law to church men's retreats without his own sons, fished with one brother-in-law, and lifted weights with the other. I've virtually adopted my wife's niece and have an excellent, if sometimes blunt, relationship with my sister-in-law.)

- Set some standards together if either of you has troublesome family members. Maybe someone calls too late, drops by unexpectedly too often, uses offensive language, or borrows things without returning them. Set boundaries so you will both be on the same page, and decide who will communicate these standards.

- Never make your wife "get her side in line." You are the head and protector of your wife. If it ever gets to the tough decisions (such as telling someone to leave or rebuking someone offensive), it falls to you, brother.

- Learn to be welcoming. You can often help your new family (and your old one) to understand how they are to treat you by reaching out first. Pursue them even when you are newlyweds, and it will establish your independence. Some in-laws don't want to impose and would welcome the invitation to spend time together.

- Learn to be flexible. This is going to be a work in progress, more than likely. Some relationships will fall into place easily, and some will not. Some may never.

- Try to avoid strife over your faith as far as it depends on you. If your in-laws are not Christ followers, you won't win them over by being a jerk about your beliefs. (Jesus' warning in Luke 12:51-53 that he would be the cause of strife even to the point of setting family members against each other was just that—a warning—not an *encouragement* to cause trouble!)

chapter nine

money: yours, mine, and ours

"We only argue about money or sex,
depending on which one is in shorter supply."

At the earliest age we are taught to share our toys. That's appropriate social behavior, no doubt. It's not until we start getting allowances that we learn that the concept ends at a cash economy. Of course, there are those rare occasions when teens might pool their money to get into a movie or concert, but it doesn't take long for the rocket scientist part of our brain to suggest, "If *I* put more in each time than Moose, then I'm actually *funding his lifestyle.*"

Thus the concept of budgeting was born. Even if that budget is rudimentary—"It's all mine and you can't have any"—at least there are rules now. This concept needs to be intelligently expanded, but it gets things rolling when it comes to understanding the value and use of money.

Most men have a control mechanism that kicks in at money and TV remotes. If you haven't gotten past the what's-mine-is-mine stage, then now would be a good time. You and your beautiful new wife are planning for the future. It's time to blend two economies for the good of a new entity, the married couple. You two have become one physically (Genesis 2:24), socially, and financially. OK, I couldn't find any Scriptures for those last two, but trust me. Sex has linked you physically and spiritually, society acknowledges you as a couple in name and status, and financially you are now sharing almost all costs and rewards.

If you are thinking that separate incomes can be kept apart, then you'd better go ahead and start a savings and loan. Then you can assign things in an efficient manner . . . and save up for the divorce you are likely headed toward. Keeping track of what each makes and owes is an unrealistic and stressful approach. This blending of money could require more communication than sex does, depending on which one is in shorter supply.

The apostle Paul wrote in 1 Timothy 5:8: "If anyone does not provide for his relatives, and especially for his immediate family, he has denied the faith and is worse than an unbeliever." The Greek word *pronoeo*, translated as *provide* there, carries the meaning of "to think of beforehand" or "foresee."

This goes way beyond finances. With you as the designated provider, it makes some sense that finances occupy a lot of your energy. This energy should be creative energy as opposed to fearful or aggressive energy. Your two incomes (if you actually have two) will need to be discussed at length, and you will discover some budget items that you don't think are worth the money—but she will. Bend a little, all-knowing one, and make sure she knows that her thoughts are being heard by you.

King Lemuel began his classic description of the wife of noble character with these words: "An excellent wife, who can find? For her worth is far above jewels" (Proverbs 31:10, *NASB*). Get that "above" part? Don't look at her as competing with your bank account.

Also consider that your wife may be a better financial

thinker than you. She may actually have an accounting degree. That would be great for most new husbands, because there are so many impulse items waiting to get you into debt. The key thing to remember here is that as the provider and environment creator, you are to provide leadership in the blending of your finances (even if you don't make as much money as your new bride, the Wall Street prodigy). It might mean you need to get out and lead a little more so you both don't default to the world's perspective that the one with the most money calls the shots. Don't abdicate leadership.

On the other hand, don't head in the opposite direction and take all the financial responsibilities upon yourself and simply hand your wife an allowance.

Listen to your wife even when it comes to big expenditures. Some women have a better perspective on using wealth for the kingdom of God than their husbands do. Consider this account from the life of the prophet Elisha:

One day Elisha went to Shunem. And a well-to-do woman was there, who urged him to stay for a meal. So whenever he came by, he stopped there to eat. She said to her husband, "I know that this man who often comes our way is a holy man of God. Let's make a small room on the roof and put in it a bed and a table, a chair and a lamp for him. Then he can stay there whenever he comes to us" (2 Kings 4:8-10).

This is the same woman to whom God miraculously gave a son after her husband was old. Then after the son died, God used Elisha to resurrect the child from death (read through v. 37). And it all started with the woman being tuned in to the spiritual dimension of Elisha, and suggesting to her husband that they add on a guest room for God's spokesman.

God intends for your marriage to be a partnership in which each person fulfills appropriate roles. Blending your finances will be easy on some points, like giving up two rents for one or combining bank accounts. That's fairly mechanical. The process of budgeting and setting goals will be the challenge. It's good to remember that you are mostly concerned with developing a habit of communication at this point, while the money issues will fall into line over a period of time.

 **to Being Awesome**

- Your wife will appreciate *some* financial planning to include *some* savings (however modest) and *some* budgeting (however painful). Combine your incomes and set shared goals. If one of you is better with accounting and wants to balance the checkbook, create a mechanism to communicate with the other how things are going. Your commitment to providing and planning ahead is what she sees, regardless of who handles what.

- Take a class together on Christian financial principles. Here are a few Christian ministries that offer excellent training and resources to help you step by step through this tricky area of finances:

  - Dave Ramsey—www.daveramsey.com

  - Crown Financial Ministries—www.crown.org

- Master Your Money by Ron Blue—www.mastermoney.org

- Focus on the Family—www.focusonthefamily.com

- Debt-Proof Living—www.debtproofliving.com

○ Set aside your personal bias of wanting to make all the decisions. If you think that's what leadership means, then you are headed for a dangerous cliff in this area. You and I aren't smart enough to do this without our wives' input and support.

○ Don't get sidetracked by immediate financial needs or conflicts. Always remember finances are dynamic and you can't expect them to just fall into place without effort and time.

○ Never force-feed a financial decision, if at all possible. It may be necessary in rare instances—like if you suddenly have to cancel a large purchase that could sink your budget—but most cases are not emergencies. You can take time to discuss and rethink all the aspects. That's important. Unresolved money issues can fester and repeat with a vengeance.

- Always place a top priority on giving to God's kingdom. Be in agreement so you will both feel like a part of what God's doing, rather than having two separate connections.

- Run from credit cards like they were soaked in disease before they were mailed out. They can take a good first year together over to the dark side before you even know it.

you don't always have to drive, but you'd better learn how to steer

"Why is *everything* with you a trust issue?"

There are two halves to a man's brain. One side says, "I don't want another responsibility" while the other side says, "I could have done that better, if you had asked me." It's a genetic thing we acquired from Adam, who, when caught *not* stepping in to protect his wife from the serpent's lies, promptly *blamed her* for his own failure to obey God's express command. He even implied that God bore some responsibility since God had given the woman to him! (Genesis 3:12). Now that's creative . . . in the worst possible sense. But it is now an inherited feature of men to delegate and then criticize later, to avoid their responsibility and later to shift blame when things go south.

Some men go to the other extreme and try to exert control over everything. These guys figure that to be safe as a leader, they'll just do all the decision making and veto everything they don't have time to figure out. This is a tough way to go, for three reasons:

1. It's not biblical.

2. It's not practical.

3. And not many women will put up with it anyway.

We had to take two cars once to see Anne's family about ninety miles away. I was to lead and she was to follow. I am not a slow driver, but I don't like to attract unnecessary legal attention—if you understand my meaning. In those days Anne was . . . well, she must have been working on her pilot's license! After twenty minutes of riding my bumper, she couldn't stand it and passed me.

Me! The leader, the husband, the one who had never (and still, as of this writing) gotten a speeding ticket. (Not that I haven't ever deserved one.) I remember how angry I was that Anne wasn't following me like we had agreed. This was in the days before cell phones, so I just fumed while she got farther out of sight.

Then I saw her pull off at a rest stop and race into the rest-room. Some leader I turned out to be! It never occurred to me that she wasn't challenging my leadership—she just had to visit the little ladies' room.

So wherein lies the balance? How do you effectively lead your wife without going to either extreme—by abdicating responsibility or by becoming a control freak? The balance lies in understanding the lack she fills in you and the design God made for being one in marriage. Looking at the original plan, man's aloneness was the only thing in creation that God pronounced "not good" (Genesis 2:18). God's solution was to "make a helper suitable for him." This means your wife fits you, and you should pay attention to her. She should be involved in everything important, since you need the insight.

You were designed to be helped! Go ahead and admit it. Get over yourself.

The tricky part begins when you recognize that your wife excels so far beyond you in some areas, you are tempted to relinquish these things over to her. But don't be too hasty in this. Your wife needs to know that she is protected by your agreement on her decisions. In other words, if you delegate an area to her, then it's your responsibility if something goes wrong. No passing the blame. Even if you agree by silence.

In speaking of women making vows, God included these instructions in the law he gave to Moses: "Her husband has the final say about any promises she makes to the LORD. If her husband hears about a promise and says nothing about it for a whole day, she must do what she said—since he did not object, the promise must be kept. But if he waits until the next day to stop her from keeping her promise, he is the one who must be punished" (Numbers 30:13-15, *CEV*).

The point here is not that a woman can't make a smart decision, but that God holds the husband responsible for covering his wife from making a mistake (and then trying to distance himself from the repercussions later).

As married men, we have been given a unique source of help, of completion, and of oneness. Even if your wife is a whole lot smarter than you and should be making all the decisions, she needs your protection. It's the payback for Adam's lack of initiative and then his shifting of blame. By including your wife in everything, then backing up her decisions, you are saying that you truly care for her.

the SMART GUY'S GUIDE to Being Awesome

- Sit down and take inventory of what areas you are both strong in. In areas that you overlap, discuss how you will make decisions so that she is right in the middle of things.

- You may want to take a personality profile test to help eliminate subjective evaluations about each other. (Don't get hung up on the fact that the theory was first identified by occultist Carl Jung. As we say in the South, even a blind hog finds an acorn once in a while.) These tests are great for easing tension areas and developing habits that account for God's makeup of each of you. Here are some resources that help assess personality types:

  - Myers-Briggs Personality Profiles—www.myersbriggs.org

  - DiSC—http://disc.unitymg.com

- Tim LaHaye's Temperament Test—www.timlahaye.com

- *Making Love Last Forever* by Gary Smalley (chapter 10 contains the animal profile test—lion/otter/beaver/golden retriever)

- *The Two Sides of Love* by Gary Smalley and John Trent

- *The Spirit-Controlled Temperament* by Tim LaHaye

● In areas where you are weak and your wife excels, agree on a way you can take the fall for her. Make sure you never blame her for failure once you've signed off on something. That's the point of protecting her.

● If she has no interest in a topic, don't just write that one off. Ask for her honest feedback, since she will almost always see things differently and you may need that new angle to decide what to do.

- Let her drive the car if she wants; there's no rule that says the man drives everywhere. It might stir up some lively discussions. Try to take notes about yourself, not her.

- On points of severe disagreement, take a few days, if possible, when you don't talk about it. Better to table the discussion in case emotions are running high, and both sides might learn something when cooled down.

- Pray over every big decision. Maybe even twice. You *might learn something.*

including a really nice parting gift

"And in conclusion, I want to remind you that
even you two will have to work to keep the magic alive."

Whether you've read this far or just skipped to the end . . . either way, I encourage you to look back over the titles of each chapter. Let these hard-learned lessons sink in for a moment. Depending on your temperament and upbringing, you will likely have a natural advantage in some of these areas. Growth in some areas will come easier than others. But no matter how well- or ill-equipped you are, each lesson must be customized to *your* wife and situation. Ultimately, she won't care what I wrote, just what you put into practice and live out.

Proverbs 28:26 says, "If you think you know it all, you're a fool for sure; real survivors learn wisdom from others" (*The Message*). We all need to constantly learn. Your Top Five list on just about any subject will not automatically match your wife's list. The brilliant idea that just popped into your head might leave her wondering how you ever qualified for Homo sapien. The things you think she's wasting time and money on might be achieving something you could never attain. And of course, vice versa, but that's all in the companion book your wife should be reading, *He's Not a Mind Reader and Other Brilliant Insights for a Fabulous First Year of Marriage: a Girl's Guide* by Brenda Garrison.

For what it's worth, please take this book as a starting point for gaining some wisdom that many of us guys—including *this* clueless guy—learned slowly and sometimes painfully.

Let it be a springboard to better lead your new wife into an amazing first year—and hopefully a lifetime.

You could start by putting the seat down.

Rules of Engagement

O K, so you've gotten to the end of this book, and by now you've probably encountered a few rough waters with your new wife. How can you successfully argue without tearing your marriage apart and ruining your sex life? (I'm just being practical here.) So glad you asked. Here are some parting words of advice that have served me well.

- Remember your mission: you are supposed to be leading toward oneness. Don't win the battle and lose the war.

- Never pull rank. OK, captain, she can read the Bible too. But just throw one good "submission" verse into a heated discussion and watch her overwhelm you with "love/gentleness/humility/sacrifice" verses back. You can't win this way. I know. (Remember the Bible compares her role to the needy-work-in-progress church, while yours should be a sacrificial role that emulates Christ.)

- It's better to win the heart and mind. No conflict really ceases unless both sides learn to trust each other. It merely simmers on the back burner, waiting to break into the open at the first thing that sets it off. Pursue that trust during the quiet times in order to avoid the conflict later.

- Know your enemy. Here's a hint—it isn't your wife. Ephesians 6:12 clearly states, "Our struggle is not against flesh and blood, but against the rulers, against the authorities, against the powers of this dark world and against the spiritual forces of evil in the heavenly realms."

- Never use a human shield. Don't blame her dad, accuse her mother, belittle her brother, or otherwise toss someone else under the bus just to win the round. And in the future when you have kids, never hang them out there to protect yourself. That is the way of a coward.

- Post a guard (over your temper). When you lose self-control, you lose credibility. No one improves any situation when he's lost his temper and starts flinging everything at the other side.

● Observe the Geneva Convention: never fight dirty. Don't lose it and get all historical, bringing up past hurts that were "forgiven," personal weaknesses shared in confidence, and comments from other people to make your point. Don't accuse, suddenly realize patterns that aren't there, and above all, don't deny truth even if it means you lose.

● Never issue an ultimatum. Words like *never, always,* and *or else* will set you up to fail if you are not willing to follow through. And if you *are* willing, you've already undermined your marriage by being a manipulator.

● Never use the doomsday weapon—The *D* word, *divorce.* If you toss that one out during an argument, even if you make up and apologize later, you've set the countdown mechanism in both your minds. You've let it be known that you haven't ruled out the "nuclear option." If you cross this line, you will be playing a game of brinkmanship (a term coined in the middle of the Cold War, and illustrated when each side seeks an advantage by threatening to push THE button first).

- Offer an olive branch at the first opportunity. End the conflict in peace as soon as possible. Be the first to give ground, the first to take responsibility, the first to apologize and change.

- Be the bigger man. Uh . . . of course, you *are* a bigger man than your wife—who is, in fact, a woman . . . Look, all I'm saying is that you are the man in this marriage. Act like it.

about the author

Jess MacCallum graduated with an art degree from the University of South Carolina, where he spent four years training with the Navigators ministry. For over twenty-nine years he has been engaged in various ministries in the church, including men's discipleship, prison Bible studies, small groups, and

marriage counseling. Jess is a business owner and the often-challenged husband of Anne, a Proverbs 31–type woman. Married for twenty-two years, Jess and Anne are the parents of three teenagers.

Jess is also the author of *I Married Wonder Woman . . . Now What?* It can be purchased at:

www.standardpub.com
www.jessmaccallum.com

Discover more brilliant insights on marriage and life in . . .

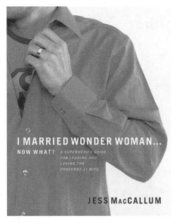

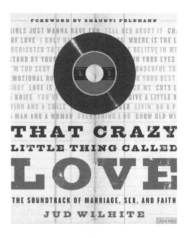

Also by Jess MacCallum!

I Married Wonder Woman . . . Now What?
Item #24312
ISBN 978-0-7847-1945-9

That Crazy Little Thing Called Love
Item #24311
ISBN 978-0-7847-1944-2

And be sure to grab this companion guide for the smart girl in your life.

He's Not a Mind Reader and Other Brilliant Insights for a Fabulous First Year of Marriage
Item #021536209
ISBN 978-0-7847-2562-7

· · ·

Visit your local Christian bookstore or
www.standardpub.com

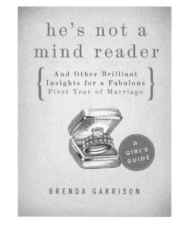

www.standardpub.com